GET CREATIVE!

The Math of Art

Written by Izzi Howell

www.worldbook.com

Co-published by agreement between Shi Tu Hui and World Book, Inc.

Shi Tu Hui
Room 1807, Block 1,
#3 West Dawang Road
Chaoyang District, Beijing 100025
P.R. China

World Book, Inc.
180 North LaSalle Street
Suite 900
Chicago, Illinois 60601
USA

© 2026. All rights reserved. This volume may not be reproduced in whole or in part in any form without prior written permission from the publisher.

WORLD BOOK and the GLOBE DEVICE are registered trademarks or trademarks of World Book, Inc.

Library of Congress Control Number: 2025942228

Aha! Academy: Math
ISBN: 978-0-7166-7377-4 (set, hardcover)

Get Creative! The Math of Art
ISBN: 978-0-7166-7386-6 (hard cover)
ISBN: 978-0-7166-7449-8 (e-book)
ISBN: 978-0-7166-7439-9 (soft cover)

Staff

Editorial

Vice President
Tom Evans

Editorial Project Coordinator
Kaile Kilner

Senior Curriculum Designer
Caroline Davidson

Curriculum Designer
Mikayla Kightlinger

Proofreader
Nathalie Strassheim

Indexer
Nathaniel Lindstrom

Graphics and Design

Senior Visual
Communications Designer
Melanie Bender

Designer
Shannon Hagman

Written by Izzi Howell

Developed with World Book by The Dream Team

Acknowledgments

The publishers gratefully acknowledge the following sources for photography. All illustrations were prepared by WORLD BOOK unless otherwise noted.

Cover: clivewa/Shutterstock; Di Studio/Shutterstock; LungMan/Shutterstock; Nelson Charette Photo/Shutterstock; phM2019/Shutterstock

© Album/Alamy Images 6; © Bridgeman Images 9, 21; © Christie's Images/Bridgeman Images 10; © PAINTING/Alamy Images 7; © Archivart/Alamy Images 19, 24; © Artefact/Alamy Images 22; © Bildagentur-online/Alamy Images 30; © Iain Masterton/Alamy Images 13; © IanDagnall Computing/Alamy Images 17, 18, 25; © Ian Paterson/Alamy Images 28; © Jan Fritz/Alamy Images 33; © JJs/Alamy Images 8; Magnus Wenninger (licensed under CC BY 3.0) 29; © Martin Shields/Alamy Images 21; © Museum of Fine Arts, Houston/gift of Texas Commerce Bancshares, Inc., Gerald D. Hines Interests and United Energy Resources, Inc./Bridgeman Images 9; © Photimageon/Alamy Images 12; Public Domain 31; Public Domain (Giovanni Battista Cecchi) 35; © Shutterstock 3, 4, 5, 6, 7, 8, 9, 10, 11, 12, 13, 14, 15, 16, 17, 18, 19, 22, 23, 25, 26, 27, 30, 31, 32, 33, 34, 35, 36, 37, 38, 39, 40, 41, 42, 43, 44, 46, 47, 48; © steeve-x-art/Alamy Images 16; © SJArt/Alamy Images 20; © UrbanImages/Alamy Images 10

There is a glossary of terms on page 48. Terms defined in the glossary are in type that looks like *this* on their first appearance on any spread (two facing pages).

Contents

Introduction 4

① **Looking at shapes** 6

    Flat on the page 8
    Think 3D 10
    Pick a pattern 12
    Tessellating tiles 14
    Super symmetry 16

② **Studying composition** 18

    The perfect shape 20
    Into perspective 22
    The golden ratio 24
    Working with scale 26

③ **Inspired by math** 28

    Mobius mysteries 30
    Impossible objects 32
    Art = math = art 34

④ **Mathematical melodies** 36

    Up the scale 38
    In harmony 40
    Rhythm and beat 42

Make a tessellating pattern 44

Index 46

Glossary 48

Introduction

Orderly, systematic math and wild, creative art may appear to have nothing in common. But if you look a little deeper, you'll start to spot mathematical ideas and rules hiding inside your favorite artworks.

And it's not just visual art! The melody and rhythm of music are also closely linked to patterns and structures straight out of a math class.

Artists use math to mix just the right color! For example, a simple green color is made by mixing blue and yellow paint in a *ratio* of 1:1.

In this book, we'll look at how math is connected to many different parts of the artistic process, from inspiration to *composition,* and see how it influences the melodies that make up the music that we all love listening to.

1 LOOKING AT SHAPES

In geometry, mathematicians look at the shape, size, and position of lines, angles, curves, and figures.

Geometry dates to the time of the ancient Egyptians and Mesopotamians. They used it to calculate distances and measure areas of land.

This ancient Egyptian papyrus looks like a modern math textbook! It contains various useful *formulas,* along with mathematical problems and solutions.

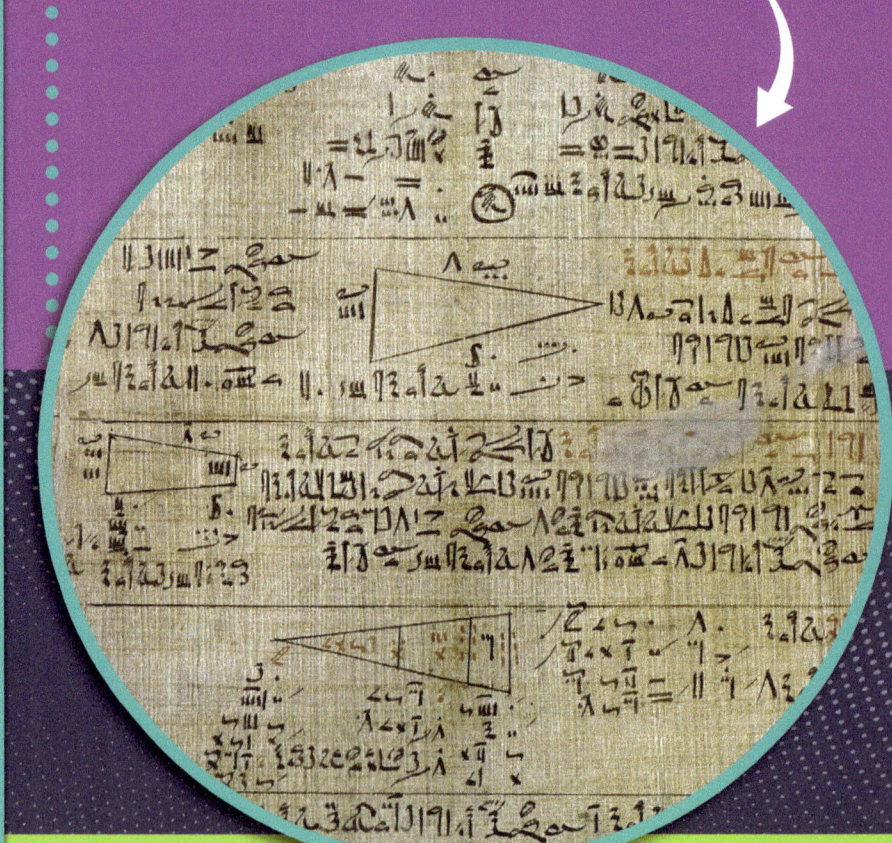

One of the most obvious crossovers between math and art is *geometry*—the study of shapes.

Geometry is used in many ways today, by engineers planning the moving parts in a machine, pilots calculating the best flight path, and architects designing a stable structure for a building.

6

However, as well as being useful, geometry can also be beautiful and striking! Artists play with geometry to create different effects in their artwork.

They can choose different 2D shapes and 3D shapes ...

... play with shapes and sequences to create patterns ...

... and experiment with *symmetry*.

Turn the page to take a closer look!

Looking at shapes

Flat on the page

First things first ... what exactly is a 2D shape? Well, the clue is in the name. A 2D shape only exists in two dimensions—length and width. It doesn't have any height to it, so it's just a flat surface.

Squares, circles, rectangles, and triangles are all examples of regular 2D shapes. Which ones can you spot in this painting by Wassily Kandinsky?

All 2D polygons have sides and corners. Round shapes don't have sides or corners, but they are often found in art.

side

corner

side

Some artists use shading to make 2D shapes pop off the page. This can create a very realistic 3D effect.

With the right use of tone, a 2D circle resembles a 3D sphere!

On a canvas, all shapes start out life as flat forms. However, that doesn't mean they have to stay that way!

In the Cubism art movement, artists broke down objects into basic 2D shapes. They wanted to show all the sides of an object, not just those that could be seen from one *perspective.*

In the painting *Femme á la guitare* by the Cubist artist Georges Braque, the scene of a woman playing the guitar is split into many different 2D shapes.

DID YOU KNOW?

There are many mathematical rules that apply to 2D shapes. For example, the sum of all the corner angles in a triangle always equals 180°.

 Looking at shapes

Think 3D

Depth • Width • Side • Height

Just like 2D shapes, most 3D shapes have edges and corners. They also have sides (which are usually regular 2D shapes).

Sculpture is probably the best-known form of 3D art. Some sculptures are representative and realistic …

… while others are **abstract**. Minimalist sculptures are often made up of very simple 3D shapes. They can be interpreted in many different ways.

Now that we've covered 2D shapes, what's a 3D shape? You guessed it! With the help of an extra dimension (depth), 3D shapes move off the page and become solid objects.

When studying irregular 3D shapes, mathematicians sometimes need to get creative. Calculating the volume of a cube is easy because there is already a *formula* that can be used.

Height × Width × Depth = Volume

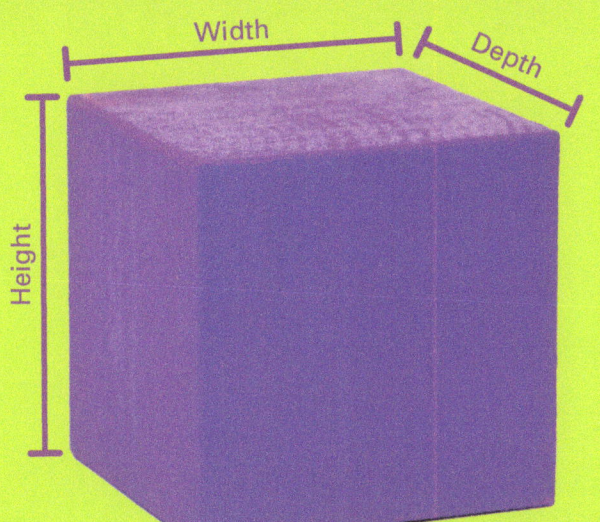

But how do you figure out the volume of a shape like this? Split the shape into smaller regular shapes, and calculate their volume, then add them all together to find the volume of the whole sculpture!

CAREER CORNER

Packaging designers use math and art skills to create new packaging for products. The packaging needs to be the correct volume to hold the product *and* look appealing, so that customers want to buy it!

⬡ Looking at shapes

Pick a **pattern**

In math, we can create number patterns by using the same rule on a set of numbers.

For example, **1, 2, 4, 8, 16, 32, 64**

In this sequence, the rule is to multiply by 2 each time.

Artists make patterns in the same way. They create rules and then follow them to produce stunning, repeated designs.

Some patterns relate to size, like the thickness of the vertical stripes in this print. There's also a repeating color pattern here—the alternating blue, black, and orange horizontal wavy lines.

Artists combine different shapes and colors to create interesting patterns. But how do they choose what order to put them in? Math, of course!

Patterns can also be found in 3D art forms, like this sculpture by Yayoi Kusama.

The bulges in the pumpkin appear at regular intervals.

The size of the dots increases and decreases in the same way all the way around.

TECH TIME

More and more scientists are now using artificial intelligence to identify patterns in their data. Machines can identify and analyze patterns much faster than humans, which helps speed up their research!

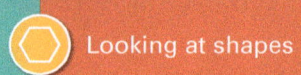 Looking at shapes

Tessellating tiles

Some of the most complex and beautiful tessellating patterns are found in ancient Islamic architecture. Buildings were decorated with brightly colored mosaic tiles arranged in tessellating patterns.

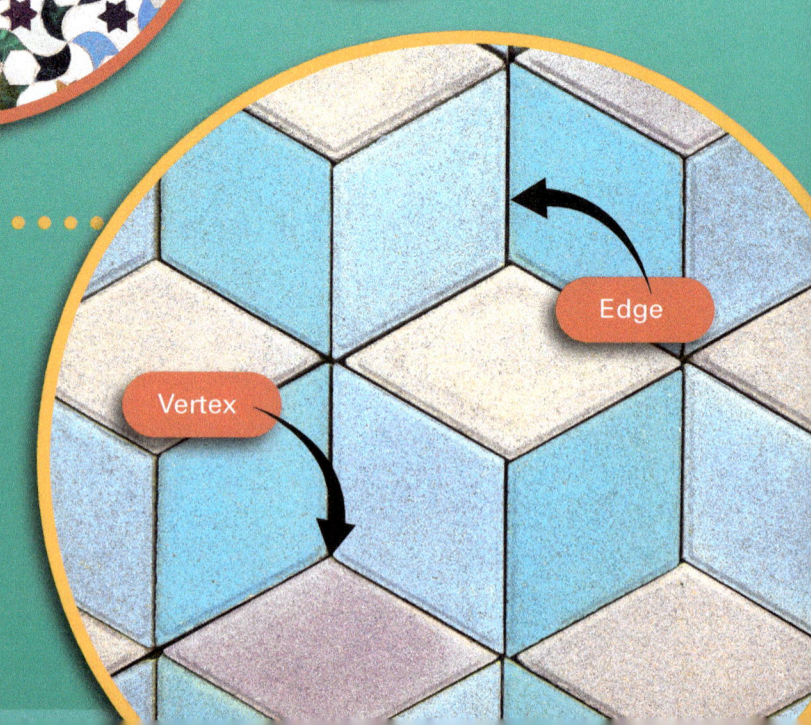

In a tessellating pattern, the border between two tiles is known as an edge. The place where three or more tiles meet is called a vertex (plural vertices).

Have you ever seen a repeating pattern of shapes that all fit together perfectly with no gaps or overlaps? This striking effect is known as *tessellation*, and it's as interesting to mathematicians as it is to artists!

Mathematicians look at a tessellating pattern and ask questions like …

How many different tessellating tile patterns are there?

How does the type of shape or shapes used affect how many shapes connect at a vertex?

What is the lowest number of colors needed to color the tiles, so that no tile is the same color as an adjacent tile?

They then create mathematical *theories* to test, and hopefully prove (!), their ideas.

CURIOUS CONNECTIONS

BIOLOGY Tessellating patterns are also found in nature, for example, the tessellating hexagons in honeycomb made by bees! Mathematicians have proven that bees use this pattern because it creates the largest volume from the smallest amount of wax.

15

Looking at shapes

Super symmetry

Reflectional symmetry is when a line of symmetry divides an object into two parts that are mirror images of each other.

This wallpaper by the artist Walter Crane has perfect vertical symmetry, creating a calm, balanced scene.

Radial symmetry is when an object looks the same after being rotated around a fixed, central point.

This Hindu mandala has a fourfold rotational symmetry. Different colors are used across the mandala to add interest, but the shapes of each section are the same.

Symmetry creates balance and striking patterns in art and is an important topic of study in *geometry.* An object is symmetrical if it can be divided into two or more identical parts.

Some artists use mathematical precision to make their works perfectly symmetrical, while others experiment with imbalance and asymmetry.

In *Under the Wave off Kanagawa,* also known as *The Great Wave,* by Katsushika Hokusai, the asymmetry of the scene emphasizes the massive size of the wave.

CURIOUS CONNECTIONS

ARCHITECTURE

Architects use symmetry to make buildings attractive and practical. Buildings are often symmetrical on the outside *and* have symmetrical floor plans inside!

Which types of symmetry can you see in these buildings? Which one is more visually interesting to you?

2
STUDYING COMPOSITION

There are lots of mathematical details and ideas that influence and shape the composition of art. Take a line, for example. This simple one-dimensional form is found everywhere in *geometry* and art. There are horizontal, vertical, zigzag, diagonal, and curved lines, to name just a few!

In composition, artists use lines to lead the viewer to the main points of interest …

Curved lines leading to the figures

Coming up with a cool pattern or a fun color scheme is only part of an artist's process. Creating a successful *composition* by choosing how and where to put things on the page is also very important!

… or to create different atmospheres …

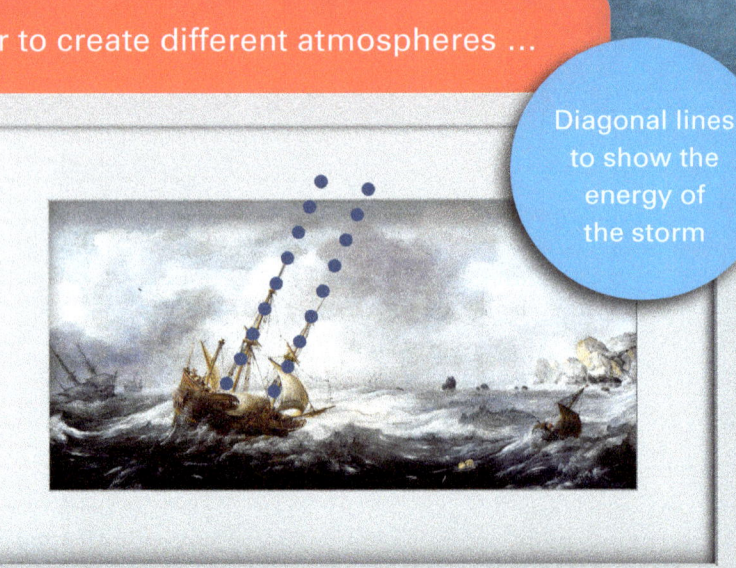

Diagonal lines to show the energy of the storm

18

... and to create lines of *perspective,* which makes art look more realistic.

Converging lines to show the depth of the room

Balancing the positive and negative space on the page is also a key part of composition.

Different *ratios* of busy and calm spaces have different visual effects.

The ratio of negative to positive space in this painting by Claude Monet is about 70:30, which gives it a calm, peaceful air.

NEGATIVE SPACE

POSITIVE SPACE

NEGATIVE SPACE

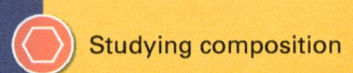 Studying composition

The perfect shape

Notice anything about the composition of *Card Players* by Paul Cezanne? That's right! The slouched backs of the players and the objects on the wall come together to create a triangular shape.

The diagonal lines of the triangular composition guide the viewer to the visual interest in the center.

As well as using geometric shapes in their artworks, artists also use *geometry* in their *composition* to balance positive and negative space.

In *Broadway Boogie Woogie*, Piet Mondrian has divided up the canvas into a grid with lots of *parallel* lines. There is visual interest across the artwork, rather than focused in one spot.

DID YOU KNOW?

Mondrian was inspired by the grid system of blocks, streets, and intersections found in New York City when painting *Broadway Boogie Woogie*.

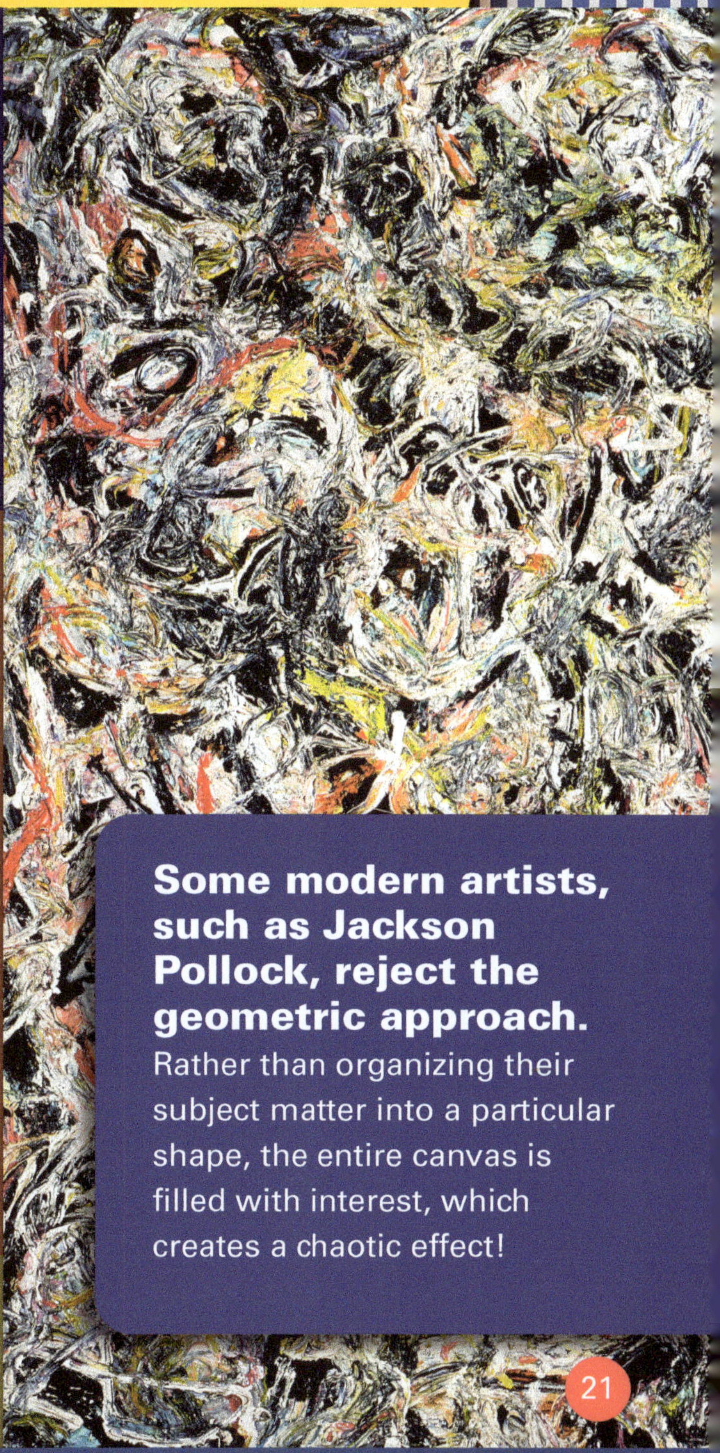

Some modern artists, such as Jackson Pollock, reject the geometric approach. Rather than organizing their subject matter into a particular shape, the entire canvas is filled with interest, which creates a chaotic effect!

21

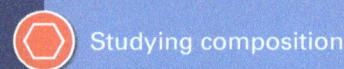
Studying composition

Into perspective

Before the Renaissance, perspective wasn't commonly used in the Western world. Artists based their *composition* on the importance of the objects in it.

During the Renaissance, mathematical *formulas* to create perspective were produced for the first time (see page 35). Ever since, artists have used these techniques to create realistic depth in their artworks.

CURIOUS CONNECTIONS

PHYSICS Earth's atmosphere also has an effect on how we see things in the distance. The way in which light is scattered through the sky makes it appear deep blue directly overhead and become lighter blue as it approaches the horizon.

Clever use of *perspective* makes some artworks look like windows into another world! This illusion is all based on *geometry* and lines.

The Rue Mosnier with Flags by Edouard Manet **is painted using linear perspective.** This effect is based on the optical illusion that *parallel* lines seem to *converge* as they get farther away.

The point where these lines would meet is known as the vanishing point.

- **In linear perspective,** distant objects are also shown smaller and closer together than nearby objects.

- **When drawing objects using linear perspective,** it can help to add guidelines that show the vanishing point(s). These lines should be drawn with a ruler for accuracy.

This cube has been drawn using two-point perspective. This means that it has two vanishing points.

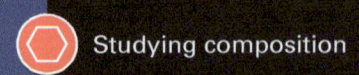

Studying composition

The golden ratio

Two quantities are in the golden ratio if their ratio is the same as their total divided by the larger quantity. Let's see that written out as an equation:

If a > b,
$$\frac{a}{b} = \frac{a+b}{a}$$

Artists often use the golden ratio to create golden rectangles. These are rectangles whose length and width correspond to the golden ratio. Golden rectangles are more pleasing to the eye than other rectangles, though no one knows why!

If you split a golden rectangle into a square and a rectangle, the length and width of the new rectangle has the same ratio as the length and width (larger dimension) of the original rectangle.

Salvador Dalí deliberately chose to paint *The Sacrament of the Last Supper* on a canvas that is a golden rectangle!

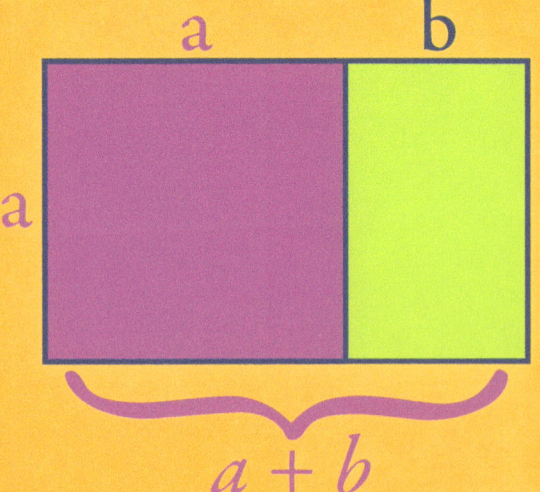

The golden *ratio* sounds mysterious and magical, but it's actually a simple mathematical pattern used by artists to balance the *composition* of their artworks!

Golden spirals get wider by the golden ratio every quarter turn that they make. Some artworks seem to follow the shape of a golden spiral, because it creates a well-balanced and interesting composition.

It seems likely that Leonardo da Vinci instinctively based the composition of the *Mona Lisa* on a golden spiral.

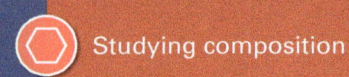

Studying composition

Working with scale

To create a maquette, an artist must first choose a scale. This is the *ratio* between the size of the maquette and the size of the final artwork. For example, a scale of 1:25 means that for every measurement of 1 inch in the maquette, the final artwork will measure 25 inches.

Before creating the full-sized version of his bronze and steel sculpture *Personage and Birds,* Joan Miró made a small wooden maquette.

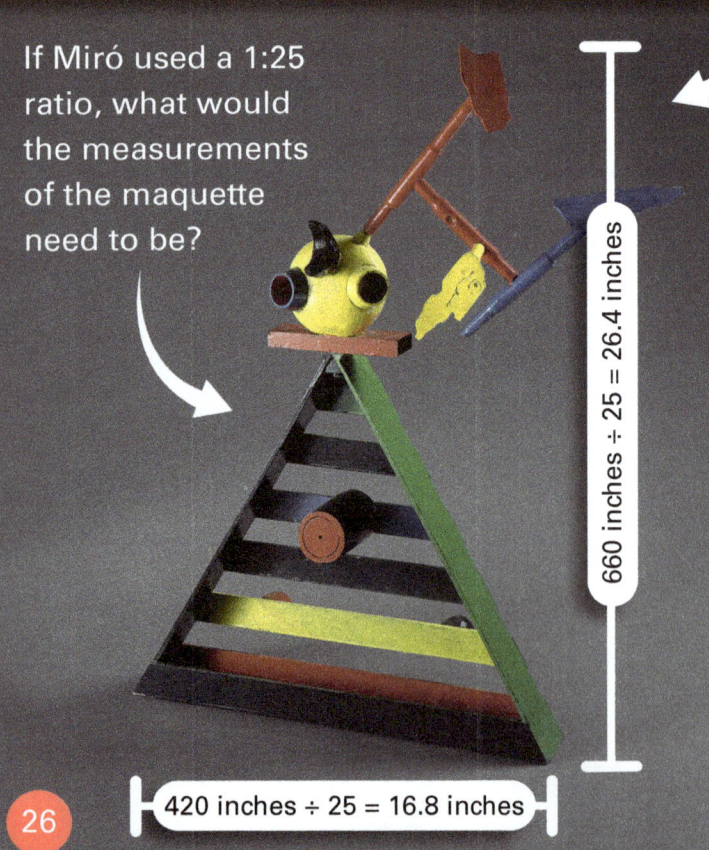

If Miró used a 1:25 ratio, what would the measurements of the maquette need to be?

660 inches ÷ 25 = 26.4 inches

420 inches ÷ 25 = 16.8 inches

CAREER CORNER

Architects need to use complex math and creative skills to design beautiful, structurally sound buildings. They use 3D printers and computer software to create incredibly accurate scale models of their buildings to present to their clients.

Artists sometimes make small models of their work known as maquettes to check the *composition* before starting the final version. They do this by using math to scale down every part of their design.

660 inches

420 inches

3 INSPIRED BY MATH

As well as using mathematical principles to guide their work, many great artists have been inspired by ideas and concepts in math. Sometimes the lines between the two fields get a little blurry!

Sometimes, artists re-create these ideas directly, like M. C. Escher's *tessellating* patterns. He created many imaginative tessellating animal patterns, after being influenced by Islamic tile design (see pages 14–15).

Other artists use mathematical concepts as a stepping off point. The sculptor Charles Perry was inspired by the twists and turns of a Mobius strip (see pages 30–31) in his sculpture *Continuum* but didn't copy them exactly.

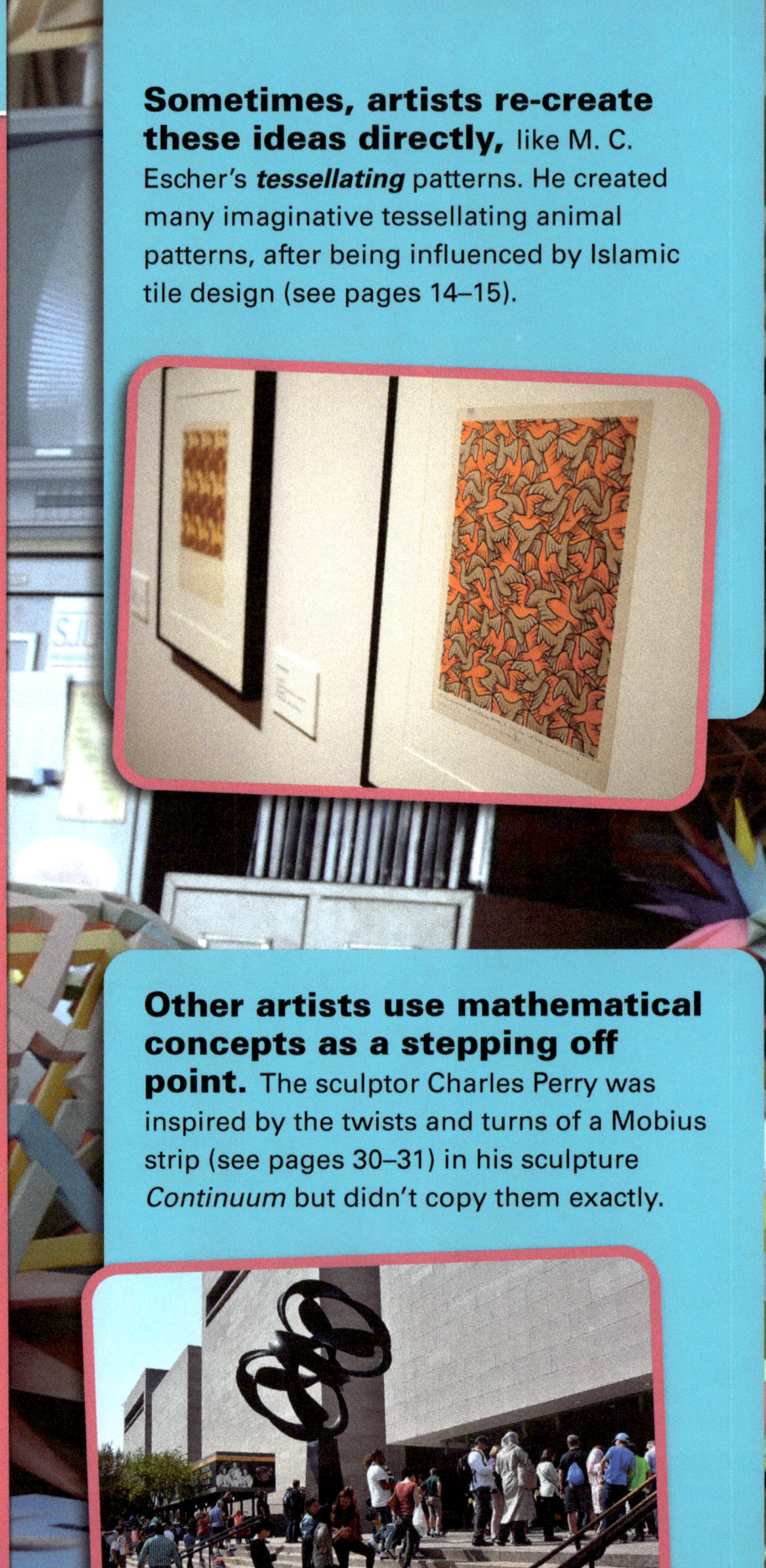

The study and expression of mathematical concepts can also be visually striking. Although these pieces weren't created by "artists," if people enjoy looking at them, perhaps they can also be considered art. What do you think?

The mathematician Magnus Wenninger created beautiful models of polyhedrons (3D forms with four or more flat faces).

Inspired by math

Mobius mysteries

The Mobius strip can be seen in many famous artworks and logos, including the recycling symbol. Because it has no end or beginning, artists use it to explore such themes as endlessness and repetition.

To fully appreciate the mysteries and marvels of the Mobius strip, it's fun to make your own! Take a rectangular strip of paper, turn over one end (twisting it 180 degrees), and join the ends.

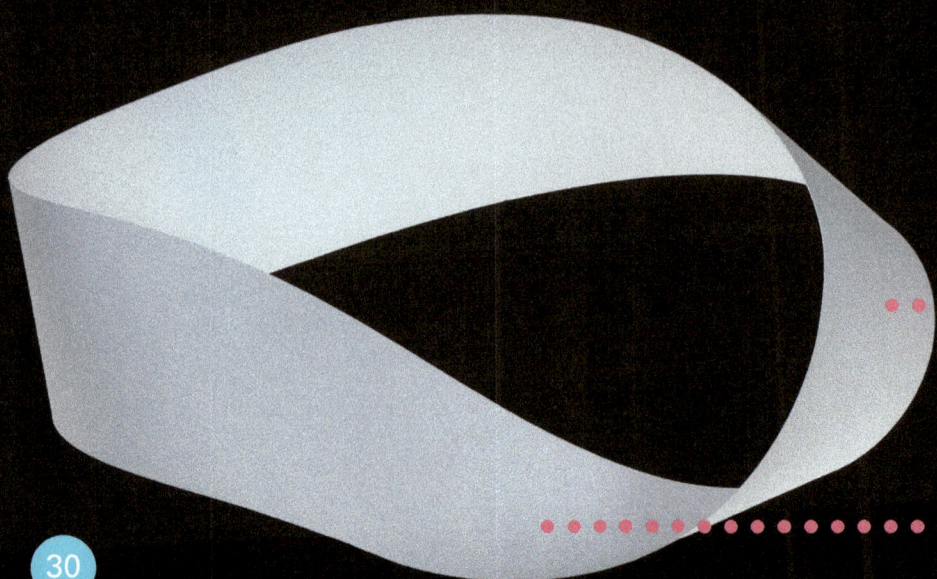

Take a look at your Mobius strip. How many sides does it have? While the original strip of paper had two sides, the new strip only has one!

How many edges does it have? That's right … only one edge, too!

The name Mobius strip may not ring any bells, but I bet you've seen one before! This curious object inspires artists and designers, as well as mathematicians.

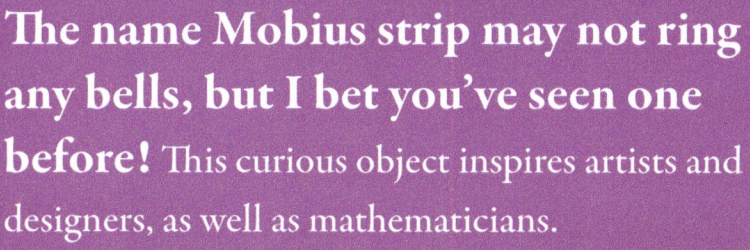

The Mobius strip is named after the mathematician who discovered it in 1858—**August F. Mobius.** However, Mobius strips can also be seen on ancient Roman mosaics from 1,500 years earlier!

The Mobius strip is an interesting object for mathematicians. They are interested in how the properties of the strip change as it is turned into a loop. This is part of a field of math called topology.

Inspired by math

Impossible objects

This is a cube, right? Check again! It's actually an impossible cube. The tangled-up edges of the cube could never come together to create a real 3D shape, but as a computer-generated image, it looks deceptively plausible!

Artists can represent impossible objects in 2D because they aren't limited by the rules of 3D construction. They use *perspective* to create an optical illusion that makes the object look real.

There are three prongs at the bottom but only two at the top!

Impossible trident

Art allows artists to explore impossible ideas that could never exist in real life, from incredible monsters to mind-bending shapes and forms. While we don't need proof that monsters aren't real, mathematicians *can* use *geometry* to explain why some objects can't exist.

Mathematicians can develop *proofs* to demonstrate that the properties of an impossible object are just that … impossible! You could also try to build one, but that might take longer!

The artist M. C. Escher is famous for his works that contain impossible objects. At first glance, parts of *High and Low* look totally normal. However, if you look more closely, you'll see that none of the floors, pillars, or staircases align as they should.

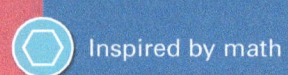 Inspired by math

Art = **math** = art

Art or math? Believe it or not, this image is actually a computer-generated graphic of a pattern of numbers, known as a Mandelbrot set. It wasn't created to be art, but it wouldn't look odd hanging in an art gallery!

Its complex, beautiful details are actually examples of a type of pattern called a *fractal*. When you zoom into a fractal image, you'll see the same patterns repeating again and again.

Art and math can both inspire each other.

Some mathematical ideas are so visually interesting that they can be considered art, while other art forms have inspired complex mathematical research.

Origami, the art of folding paper into decorative objects, has influenced several mathematical studies, including how one square piece of paper can be folded to create different shapes …

… and research into the angles and shapes in the crease patterns left behind on the paper after making an origami model.

Which 2D shapes can you see in this crease pattern?

During the Renaissance, the Italian architect **Filippo Brunelleschi** started to study the angles and lines that created the illusion of *perspective.* He painted scenes *and* came up with the mathematical calculations needed to produce the visual effect. It's hard to say which came first … the art or the math!

④ MATHEMATICAL MELODIES

1, 2, 3, 4 … even before a piece of music begins, its connection to math is clear.

A conductor uses their hands to count the beat of the music, so that the musicians start playing at the same time and at the same speed.

Visual arts are not the only art form that are influenced by mathematical ideas. Mathematical patterns, rules, and *formulas* also shape the songs we love to play and listen to.

The musicians in a band often play different rhythms on their instruments. These patterns are made by playing notes for different lengths of time, which can be expressed as mathematical fractions (see page 43).

Math also affects the notes on an instrument. They must be tuned to the correct *frequency*, so that the *ratio* between the notes is correct (see pages 38–39).

Many of the same mathematical concepts we see in art can also be found in music. For example, just as images can be reflected to create a mirror image, melodies can be "inverted" so that the notes change position.

37

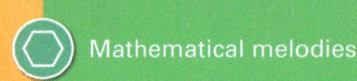

Mathematical melodies

Up the scale

Most music is based on a scale—a set of tones or notes. The natural notes in a scale are named C, D, E, F, G, A, and B. The names of the notes then repeat again.

A note can also be raised or lowered slightly in *pitch* to produce a tone halfway between it and the note next to it. The halftone above a note is called its ***sharp*,** and the halftone below a note is called its ***flat*.**

DID YOU KNOW?

On a piano, natural notes are played on the white keys, and sharps and flats are played on the black keys.

Who are you calling flat?!

+1/12 an octave

C D E F G A B C

Ever wondered why the notes in a scale sound *just right?*

Behind the music is a simple number pattern ... let's take a look!

The distance between one note and the next highest note with the same name is called an octave. *Frequency* doubles between one octave and the next, so the *formula* to figure out the rise in pitch is 2n.

Usually, the 12 notes in an octave are spaced out evenly. This means that the *ratio* between each note is ¹⁄₁₂ the width of an octave. This creates a steady rise in pitch throughout.

Sounds good to me!

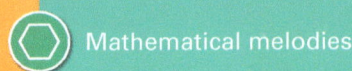

Mathematical melodies

In harmony

Two or more notes played together at the same time is known as a chord. The distance between each note is known as the interval. When the interval between notes in a chord follows a certain pattern, the notes are in harmony with each other.

The most common type of chord is the *triad*, which consists of three notes, each with an interval of three scale degrees.

This triad contains the notes C, E, and G.

C

E

G

+3 scale degrees

Why do some notes sound great when played together, and others sound clashing and wrong? The secret? Harmony! And the secret to harmony? That's right—it's math!

This mathematical pattern of intervals can be used to create harmonious chords in any scale! Just start at a different note, and copy the intervals!

Some composers experiment with other intervals to create different musical effects. Some combinations may sound dissonant (rough and unpleasant) to certain people.

According to legend, the Greek mathematician **Pythagoras** observed that different blacksmiths' hammers made different sounds as they hit the anvil. Some hammers sounded harmonious together, while others didn't. After investigating the weight of the hammers and the sounds they produced, Pythagoras discovered that if the weight of the hammers formed a whole number *ratio,* striking them at the same time would sound pleasant!

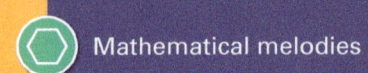

Mathematical melodies

Rhythm and **beat**

The shape of a note tells musicians how long it should last.

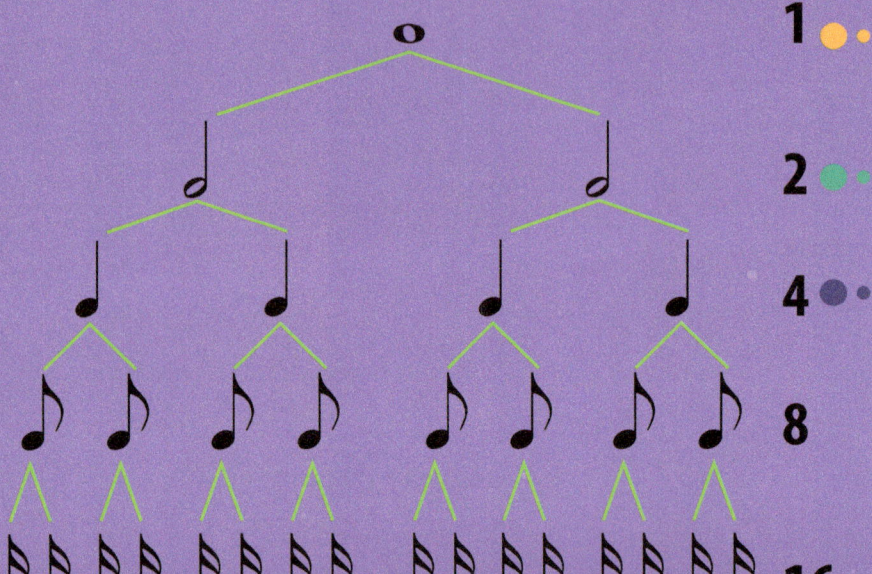

- **1** — The whole note has the longest time value of any note normally used.
- **2** — You can halve a whole note to make half notes ...
- **4** — ... and then continue dividing the duration of the note by 2 to get quarter notes, eighth notes, and so on.
- **8**
- **16**

The time signature of a piece of music tells musicians how many of each type of note are in each measure, or bar. For example, in the time signature 4/4, there are four (the top number) quarter beats (the bottom number) to a measure.

Rhythm and beat lie at the heart of music,

moving the melody forward at a steady but interesting pace. As we saw on page 37, it's all thanks to fractions that these musical patterns fit together so perfectly!

However, this doesn't mean that you can only use quarter beats in the rhythm!
Composers use fractions to find out other combinations of notes that could fit in the same measure.

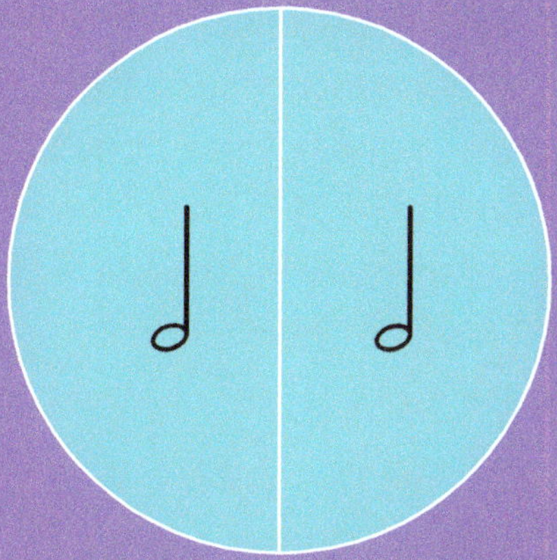

Two half notes

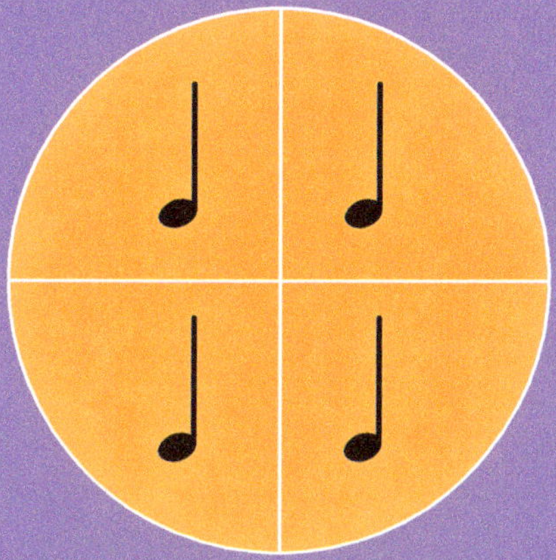

Four quarter notes

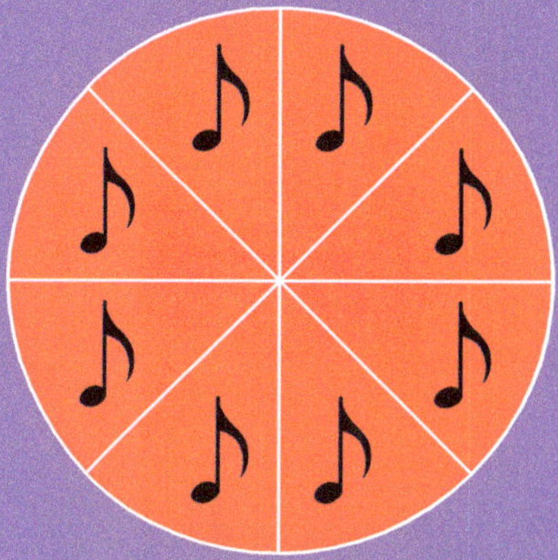

Eight eighth notes

Or why not use a variety of fractions to vary the rhythm even more!

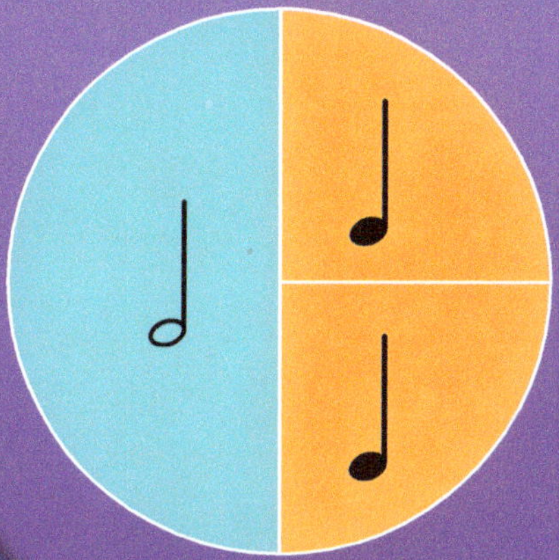

One half note and two quarter notes

Three quarter notes and two eighth notes

Make a **tessellating** pattern

You will need:
- A ruler
- A pencil
- Thin cardboard
- Scissors
- Tape
- Paper
- Art supplies of your choice (pens, pencils, markers, paint, etc)

Give it a try

1. Use the ruler and the pencil to draw a 2-inch square on the cardboard, and then cut it out.
2. Turn your square diagonally as shown below. Use the pencil to draw a line from the bottom corner of the square to the left-hand corner, and then another line from the bottom corner to the right-hand corner. This could be a curve, a zigzag, or whatever you feel like!

Combine your math and art skills to create an incredible *tessellating* pattern! Be inspired by the designs on pages 14–15, or use your creativity to come up with something modern and new!

3. Cut along the line that connects the bottom corner to the left-hand corner (shown here in red). Take this piece and stick it to the opposite side of the square using tape. Now repeat the process with the other line.

4. Draw around your template on the paper using a pencil. Once you've finished one shape, line up your template so that it fits perfectly against the drawn shape, and draw another one! Finally, add color to your tessellating pattern.

Try this next!

Can you design a tessellating pattern made up of two different shapes? Make some different templates, and see how they can combine. Remember, your design can't overlap or have any gaps!

QUESTION TIME!

As you may remember from page 15, mathematicians often come up with *theories* about tessellations and color. Put their question to the test, and see if you can figure out the minimum number of colors needed, so that no tile is the same color as an adjacent tile.

45

Index

A

ancient Islamic art, 14, 28
angles, 6, 9, 35
architecture, 6, 14, 17, 26, 35

B

Braque, Georges, 9
Brunelleschi, Filippo, 35

C

Cezanne, Paul, 20
chords, 40, 41
color, 5, 12, 13, 15, 16, 18, 45
composition, 5, 18–27
convergence, 19, 23
Crane, Walter, 16
Cubism, 9

D

Dalí, Salvador, 24
Da Vinci, Leonardo, 25

E

Escher, M. C., 28, 33

F

formulas, 6, 11, 22, 36, 39
fractals, 34

G

geometry, 6, 7, 17, 18, 21, 23, 33
golden ratio, 24–25

H

harmony, 40–41
Hindu art, 16
Hokusai, Katsushika, 17

I

impossible objects, 32–33
intervals, 13, 40, 41

K

Kandinsky, Wassily, 8
Kusama, Yayoi, 13

L

lines, 6, 12, 16, 18, 19, 20, 21, 23, 35

M

Mandelbrot set, 34
Manet, Edouard, 23
maquette, 26, 27

Miró, Joan, 26, 27
Mobius, August F., 31
Mobius strip, 28, 30–31
Mondrian, Piet, 21
Monet, Claude, 19
music, 36–43

N
notes, 37, 38, 39, 40, 41, 42, 43

O
octaves, 39
origami, 35

P
patterns, 5, 7, 12–13, 14, 15, 17, 25, 28, 34, 35, 36, 37, 39, 40, 41, 43
perspective, 9, 19, 22–23, 32, 35
pitch, 38, 39
Pollock, Jackson, 21
Pythagoras, 41

R
ratios, 5, 19, 24, 25, 26, 37, 39, 41
Renaissance, 22, 35
rhythm, 37, 42, 43

S
scale, 26–27
scales (musical), 38–39, 40, 41
sculptures, 10, 13, 26, 28

symmetry, 7, 16–17

T
tessellation, 14–15, 28, 44–45
3D shapes, 7, 8, 10–11, 13, 26, 29, 32
time signatures, 42
2D shapes, 7, 8–9, 10, 11, 32, 35

V
vanishing points, 23
volume, 11, 15

Glossary

abstract (AB strakt)—describes a type of art that doesn't try to represent the appearance of people or things

composition (KOM puh ZIHSH uhn)—the arrangement or design of an object

converge (kuhn VURJ)—to come together to meet at a point

formula (FAWR myuh luh)—a mathematical rule expressed in numbers and letters or words

fractal (FRAK tuhl)—a geometric shape containing a never-ending, repeating pattern

frequency (FREE kwuhn see)—the number of times that a sound wave is produced within a period

geometry (jee OM uh tree)—the branch of mathematics that measures and compares lines, angles, surfaces, and solids in space

parallel (PAR uh lehl)—always the same distance apart and never meeting

perspective (puhr SPEHK tihv)—the technique of giving depth to a 2D image

pitch (pihch)—how high or low a sound is

proof (proof)—the calculations that show how the solution to a mathematical problem was reached

ratio (RAY shee oh)—the relation between two numbers

symmetry (SIHM uh tree)—having two or more parts that match exactly

tessellation (TEHS uh LAY shuhn)—fitting shapes together in a regular pattern with no gaps in between

theory (THEE uhr ee)—an explanation based on thought and reasoning

www.ingramcontent.com/pod-product-compliance
Lightning Source LLC
Chambersburg PA
CBHW061251170426
43191CB00041B/2412